Lets Start A Business

By Matthew James

Dedication

For my husband who believed in me when I needed it most. I could spend the entire book writing about how your support helped me achieve so much and without you I would not have been able to do anything, I just hope others have someone like you to fight in their corner like you did for me.

For my Fleur Bear, the dog I always wanted for so long and finally got! I know you cannot read this, but I want you to know you are loved. I love you both always xxx

Copyright

Contents

Introduction

"Success is no accident. It is hard work, perseverance, learning, studying, sacrifice and most of all, love of what you are doing or learning to do."

I am not interested in any way about football, but this quote from Pele sums up what starting a small business is all about. You need to accept that to be successful, you are going to have to put in the work to achieve it.

All businesses start based on an idea, a concept or even an initial thought process for the groundwork that a business is built from. It is the same process for all types businesses, big or small there must be a person with an idea for it to start with. If you have an idea for a business but are not sure where to start to move forward, then this is the book for you.

I shall start by stating that starting a business is not easy and running a business is not easy. I feel like that needs to be put in bold and underlined so you can appreciate how much I need to stress that running a business is so difficult. If you are considering a small business, a side hustle or something you can expand upon into something bigger, they all start the same. Each business will also go through the same sort of trials and tribulations and will face difficult times.

Mentally, physically, and obviously financially starting a business is exhausting. It is not an easy thing to do (even if you are thinking of it as a small side business) and that is just to start with. The process takes a long time, requires hard work to begin with, during and after your initial idea to start something and make it a success.

This book is about my experience as a small business owner, I will be honest and precise as possible while btrying to keep a light hearted tone. There will be six chapters and six steps to starting a business, which I will go through with you to start a business like I already have. There is a blank business plan for you to use, I will also include the one I used to start my escape room business so you can see the real-life example.

If you can accept all that and are ready for the huge challenge ahead then Let's… Start A Business!

About The Author:

I am 34, a husband and a proud dog dad. I currently live in the North East of England with my husband and our 3-year-old Staffordshire bull terrier named Fleur, whom we rescued last year and it has been a joy getting to know her.

We spend our days either in the garden, walking the dog and enjoy reading or binge watching the latest shows on Netflix. I like being creative, though I do not really feel I am talented at it, yet still I like try most arts and crafts. I of course like to write and business in general.

I have had a good life and have achieved a lot in my 34 years which may seem young to some, but every day I feel I am constantly learning, trying to improve and make things better for myself and my family.

For most of my life I have been involved in business – my parents owned a fish and chip shop when I was 10 years old and I loved working there, as I got to see the banter my dad would have with customers and how my mum complimented his style by being caring to those who came in. At first, I thought my dad was being unprofessional joking around and speaking to people in such an informal way, but I soon realised he was delivering great customer service – keeping people entertained as they waited for fish and chips. Not only were the fish and chips excellent quality but my parents ensured the service was excellent too. It was clever really – fish was cooked to order so there would usually be a 5 minute or so wait for most customers and the time was filled with my dad's banter. Plus, my mum was great with keeping up with the locals and their families. I was only young but understood quickly what people were coming in for – it was not just the tasty fish and chips.

Recently a lot of people have asked me after selling my business, what it is I will go on to do next. The answer I give them is that I do not know. I never knew I wanted to start a business in the first place let alone start 3 different ones and achieved success with them, something I thought was not possible. In business, such as everything in life, I feel like each idea has an expiry date. By that, I mean a business idea will go through a lifespan from idea to creation to closing. Nothing lasts forever, just make sure you enjoy it while it does last.

I feel like if you have got a firm idea for a business and you are willing to work hard to achieve it, anything is possible. Try not to listen to others who tell you negative things. There is a place for constructive criticism but when starting a business, you need to be mentally strong to succeed.

If you wish to contact me, need some help or advice, I would be happy to discuss over email, I would love It if you enjoyed this book and it helped you, to let me know!

letsstartasomething@gmail.com

Find me on Instagram – @Letsstart.abusiness

My experience in business

I have had several small businesses, right from "Helping Hands," the business I setup with my brother when I was ten years old to more recently (and most successfully) an escape room business.

I studied business studies at school, along with marketing at college. I also had a placement at a local enterprise agency after leaving college. I will say that I am not an expert or qualified in business like others are, I have only my experience to show, which I thought a lot of potential business owners could benefit from.

My first success in business was an American Sweet Shop I opened in a small seaside town where I then lived. It was a time when buying American sweets was popular and big supermarkets had not started selling similar items. I opened the shop on a very tight budget, relying on friends financially and family to help me. This meant the shop had very little stock to begin with, but I expanded the ranges quickly and was able to order in more ranges, eventually able to stock Australian sweets as well as American.

Part of the success was due to a very engaged Facebook page – reaching over a thousand likes quickly (I often ran competitions to grow the page and to keep people engaged) but also the shop was located on a busy area near the seafront. I was able to make the money back I had borrowed as well as some profit too. But problems started when other (bigger) businesses started to stock similar products at cheaper prices. In short, the market changed in as little as 6 months. It went from American sweets being different and found in very few shops to being made available almost everywhere and at cheaper prices I could never match or beat. Thank you very much, Tesco.

Also, a contributing factor (I am happy to admit it was my mistakes for the decline of the business but these listed reasons are some of the events that led up to the closure) was how Facebook changed for businesses. No longer were posts being seen by everyone in a timeline, they were being shown in terms of engagement and popularity. Most of my business came from Facebook, so my posts no longer reaching a wide audience, meant fewer people were coming to the shop. I had regular customers who were great but something had changed and was not for the better. Sure, it could be a coincidence, but I do feel these were the key reasons that lead to the decline in business.

I decided to close the shop when sales began to decline and the landlord wanted me to sign a longer lease. I thought I could make an online shop work and no longer need to rent any space, but the website did not take off. There are many reasons for this but mainly due to my own lack of knowledge of digital marketing, advertising, and making a website work. I gave up on the idea of American sweets being a viable business and instead went back into the world of employment in sales and retail. But it would not last, you may find that once you have been self-employed, it is difficult to find a job that replaces that buzz, that joy of earning money for yourself.

My biggest success as a small business owner started in 2018. My partner and I enjoyed doing escape rooms (sort of Crystal Maze style challenges where players were supposedly locked inside a room and had one hour to solve puzzles to escape in the time limit) and I thought that I could make it work as a new business venture.

I quit my job at the time and opened my own escape room, I created all puzzles for the room, decorated the rooms, and the website for the business. I ran the games (meaning I was there practically 24/7 watching teams attempt to solve the puzzles and helped when needed) and marketed the escape rooms myself. This time I had a better understanding of websites and digital marketing and the escape room business was a huge success. I loved it.

I expanded quickly, opening another escape room with a different theme but needed help from my partner in order to run it. The business was making good profit which I used to make further rooms – including a Christmas themed pop-up escape room each year. Eventually I had 3 different rooms and a different Christmas one to boot.

Each room had enough challenging puzzles (all created by my partner and I) locks and surprises along the way. With each room came new ideas, electronic puzzles (where players would need to do something for the lock to be released) and more immersive experiences. Customer expectations were high and getting higher as escape rooms in the UK became more well known and more escape room businesses were opening.

The escape rooms were very successful, we had wonderful returning players that made it feel like I was hanging out with friends, rather than work. We had nothing but positive reviews over trip advisor and google reviews, as well as many positive Facebook recommendations (over 400).

Yet there was a big downside to the business, in between looking after players I was frantically trying to build new rooms, to give bigger and better experiences for players and it came with a high price. It meant me being away from my partner and practically living at work, day, and night. It got to the point where I would be there from 8am in the morning until late at night only coming home to eat and sleep. It took its toll on me and my partner as well as our relationship. He was already having to come in and help on Saturdays, as well as working full time and studying on top.

I needed to employ staff for the first time ever as I could not carry on working all hours, I was burnt out and that was with my partner helping me on a Saturday. I found someone suitable and began the process of training them.

But then the pandemic hit. Escape rooms (along with all other businesses) were forced to close. With no players, it meant no business! Great!

I carried on during the pandemic, making virtual escape rooms on a website for players instead. I was one of the first (to my knowledge) to open an online escape room and many others came after it. The games were automated and self-service meaning I did not need to clue players or guide them when playing.

Once again, the business was successful and migrated online with the same enthusiasm from players but it was also still personally exhausting – creating online games was easier than creating new physical rooms, but with each new set of rules that came into force, I still did not have any idea when I would be able to open and, in the meantime, still paying all bills on the building I rented for the business.

Towards the end of the pandemic, we were finally able to open and have players come in person – but I was burnt out. I had had enough of working all the time and luckily my partner gained a new job that required us to move to the North East. I was able to sell the business and we purchased our first home together.

If you are still with me, good job. I am finally getting towards the present!

When we moved, I decided to try and carry on with escape rooms in a different format – boxed escape rooms to play at home. It did not work as well and while I managed to sell quite a few units, but like American Sweets, escape rooms had moved on with players expecting more than a puzzle leading to a code to unlock a padlock formula.

I decided to take a break from doing a business, using my time to decorate our new home instead.

Yet, like many other business owners, I missed being busy and felt the need to start something else. We had recently converted to becoming vegetarian and whenever we wanted a takeaway, we found there were serious lack of options...

I opened a vegan takeaway after studying for a level 2 in food hygiene and researching into the vegan way of cooking. I created a full website for orders, menu, and all the dishes. I ran competitions on social media to help gain followers and posted as nice pictures as I could of the food on Instagram.

It was successful on a much smaller scale (I was open just weekends after deciding that I did not want to make the same mistake as working all the time like with the escape rooms) and I enjoyed being able to create new dishes, working in a kitchen and doing a different type of business.

Sales began to decline after a while and I decided that because we lived in a small area, the business would not be able to grow unless we moved so I closed it recently. I feel all things have a lifespan and some of my businesses have lasted longer than others but each one has been on my own terms.

Now, I decided to write this book to help others in business, to go over my mistakes as well as successes in an honest and informative way. I have devised six steps to start your own small business whilst also sharing what a real business would do in each step to show what you need to do to succeed. Right, enough about me, Let's... Start A Business!

How To Use This Book:

This book is intended for those looking to start a business and not sure where to begin as a startup or you could be a business owner looking for some hints and tips. I will also include a blank business plan template for you, this includes cashflows that will automatically populate when being filled in. I will use this same business plan from my own escape room business so you can see what has been used in a real business scenario too.

Each chapter is a step you will need to take in order to start your business journey – from initial concepts (see Chapter 1, Step 1 – Where To Start) right through to launching a business (Chapter 6 – Step 6: Launch). With 6 chapters in total.

You can use this book in any way you need, but I suggest even when you have set your business up, to refer to the business plan and even adjust based on your new objectives / goals (more in chapter 6) for the business going forward.

There are summaries at the end of each chapter, this is where you should put into practice of what you have learnt from this book. It will give you an overview of the chapter too.

At the back of the book is a glossary if you are unsure of any the words / terms mentioned. I will try and keep acronyms to a minimum (even though, like everything else they do pop up) and I shall try to use easy to read language. You will also find links and a glossary at the back of the book and lists of websites / apps I use.

Using a real-life example

I am going to use each step to start a business so you can see how the full process works. This business is called **Let's Start An Escape Room Business**! It will be based upon the real-life examples I used to start my escape room business in 2018 and even use the same business plan I used to launch the business. This is not the business name I used, I have decided not to name it or the location (in the business plan, I use "the city" for example as to where) due to the business still being up and running after I sold it.

Chapter 1: Step One – Where To Start

This can be the difficult area for a lot of people. You want to start a business but not sure which direction to go in? Or what service or products to sell?

It can be a daunting to start with and one of those type of decisions that is yours to make.

I will say here, right away, people will be negative about your business. They may mean well, but they will have "ideas" and "thoughts" about what it is you are trying to do. It can be very difficult to stay positive but you need to accept this and rise above it.

My own parents said to me that my first business I did would fail. Those were their actual words – that it would fail. Now, at the time I was not in the best place mentally and my confidence was at a low. So, to have them say that on top of trying to figure out how to make a business work, was not helpful to say the least. I respected my parents as they had run fish and chip shops and sort of introduced me to the world of business.

Friends and family may be more supportive but I guarantee most of your friends and family will share a few posts for your business on social media and then stop doing so. I do not know why people do this but maybe some people think you starting a business is about gain for yourself. Which, to an extent it is. Yet their help and support, throughout will make things a lot easier. Trust me when I say that not everyone will be supportive as you think!

My first piece of advice is to use lists as in writing down everything – I know it sounds odd, but if you write down everything you need to do, it will help. It can keep you motivated and grounded. I use lists for everything I do in life – from what I need to complete in the day, to regular stuff like shopping but also all my thoughts and business ideas. I keep them on the notes app on my phone – that way I can always add to it as soon as an idea or something I need to do comes into my head. The process of setting yourself a to do list and getting it finished for the day breaks down short term and longer-term goals.

For example, starting a business will feel like endless things to do and can be overwhelming. But if you break it down into goals and what you need to do to achieve those goals in smaller tasks, it will really help overall.

Research

You need to thoroughly research into your potential business idea. This will include knowing your products (including any health and safety issues) knowing your market you intend to sell to and where you will be selling.

Money will play a key part in starting a business. Your financial situation will be pushed to its limits – if you have a lot of money to start up with, you will still need to plan and work out everything correctly for your business to succeed. If you do not have a lot of money for the initial investment, you can still achieve success in business on a tight budget. You need to think creatively, plan everything and ensure your costings / profit / loss are correct. It's worth planning for every hypothetical situation financially too – such as what if you make no sales in the first month of trading and you have a shop to pay bills for? Keeping a tight grip on finances is one of the keys to success in business. Ensure you have enough money to start up with, some for backup and to continue with into your business journey.

You can gain financing through loans, savings if you have them, raising funds via crowd funding (where you use a platform on the internet for people to give funding to you in order to reach specific goals) or if you have friends and family willing to back you financially. It is so important to consider your finances and knowing where you will get the money from to start your business. This is not easy – how much money will you need? What if you need more than you can borrow? The best way to tackle finances is to fill in the cashflows in a business plan (lucky for you a blank business plan and filled in one is in chapter 4) and budget as best as you can through your research into your business.

Let us say you are looking to open a pizza shop. A basic list of the costs you will incur when starting this business will be:

- Rent
- Bills
- Insurance
- Signage
- Flyers / menus
- Kitchen equipment including pizza ovens
- Ingredients
- Packaging
- Pizza delivery vehicle
- Till / Card machine
- Telephone
- Website

This might be a very rough and basic list but shows what you would need to research into. Plus, you will need spare finances for contingencies.

Most start-up businesses will start by referring to the Marketing Mix: known as the Seven Ps. These are 7 objectives or goals that you need to form a business:

Product: (or service) what will you be selling? Will you buy products from a supplier or make yourself? Is there a need for your product / service or is the market already flooded with similar products or services. Tied this in with USP (Unique Selling Proposition) meaning your product or service need to have something that stands out, makes it different to what is already available. This could be starting a business on a specific niche (such as dog accessories aimed at owners of a specific breed like Dachshunds) or make your product / service have something extra that your competitors do not. For example, if you have a gardening business and, in your area, there are 5 other existing businesses, could you offer something extra or even free on top of an existing service? Such as, including free mowing of front yard if purchasing back yard cut. Compare your prices, products and services with existing businesses and think creatively as to how yours can be made different.

Your product or service must comply to health and safety regulations – be sure to check on this first before you do anything else. You may need to start with a prototype if inventing something new, which can cost a lot to be made (unless making something yourself).

Price: This may seem obvious but setting your prices correctly not only means you will make a profit but also can determine whether your customers will buy from you or not. Too expensive and they will go elsewhere, too cheap and they may consider your product / service to be sub-par. You need the correct balance which can never be easy.

Pricing your goods or services is not easy, and there is no single rule to follow which will give you the correct price. This is one simple way to try and cost up a good for sale. Remember you will likely need to adjust this for your own circumstances;

Firstly, you need to work out your expected fixed costs. This includes items such as rent, overheads or other expenditure. The key here is that these costs remain the same, regardless of the number of items you sell.

Secondly, you need to work out your variable costs (also known as marginal costs). A variable cost is the cost of producing/selling one unit, such that if you sold two units, it would cost you twice the amount of variable costs than if you sold one.

Next, you need to estimate the number of goods you are predicting to sell. This should be in line with your business plan and cashflow projections. Then divide the total (annual) fixed costs by number of items you expect to sell. Add this amount to the variable cost of selling one. This will give you the estimate the cost of production/sale of one item. You will then need to factor in your profit margin/mark-up, to calculate your final price.

An example of this method is shown below. Of course, it is likely you will have more than one good or service for sale, so will need to consider this when allocating your costs.

		Per month	Per year	Per item
Fixed Costs	Rent	£625.00	£7,500.00	
	Bills	£100.00	£1,200.00	
	Insurance	£100.00	£1,200.00	
	Other	£350.00	£4,200.00	
	Total		£14,100.00	
Expected number of sales			1,040	
	Fixed cost per sale			£13.56
Variable Costs	Cost of purchase			£2.50
Total cost per sale				£16.06
Profit per sale				£3.94
Sale Price				£20.00

If you are ordering stock, or even tools for your service, ensure you remember to include everything in your price you charge customers. I once read a post on a catering Facebook group from someone comparing their price of a bacon sandwich and what others charge for the same. This is a bit silly in my opinion – only you will know how much your ingredients cost you and what time and effort go into making this sandwich for example. Factor in the costs for you to get the ingredients, your time and worth. It is all well and good others saying they charge £4 for their sandwich but what you charge will be with all the other factors of costs added in. On the flip side, of course you cannot just charge thousands of pounds for something which has a ceiling price. Best way is to gauge what others charge in your local area or if you are online and completely niche, seek other websites for rough costings, plus your cost / time as mentioned already.

With pricing, you may feel you need to discount in order to gain business – this is not necessarily all that influences a customer decision whether to buy from you or not, so do not be quick to lower prices. The same goes for customers stating they can find the same product cheaper elsewhere – you do not have to match that price or change your prices to be cheaper, stick to your pricing as you see fit. I often had customers moan about my prices in my American sweet shop – it was expensive for me to export American sweets from America and my prices were a lot lower than other similar shops. But when Tesco and other supermarkets could buy the same products in bulk at lower prices, I could never compete with their buying power, something customers failed to comprehend.

Promotion: Another key element to all businesses, how will you promote your product / service to gain business or even keep existing customers to return for more? It is an objective that you should keep ongoing. Simply opening a shop and opening the doors will not bring customers in. There's digital advertising (online, on social media) or physical advertising such as leaflets, handing out in person.

Every business needs promotion in order to survive. If you look at celebrities, they promote everything all the time, from fashion in clothes they wear, to beauty products, haircare and more. They do this via social media, or when on tv – as well as promoting their book / film etc

This is an example of cross promotion, in business terms this would be done by promoting a product (let us say via Facebook Sponsored posts) and if a customer goes to purchase on your website, your website would also suggest a related product. Like, selling a games console and then cross promoting a memory card to go with it. (not that they need memory cards anymore except for the Nintendo Switch)

Place: This needs to be carefully considered and links in with the other Ps. You need to think of not only is the location good for customers to get to (and accessible to all), but also for deliveries of stock.

Is there a similar business located nearby? What is the footfall like? What about parking? If you are planning of starting a business from home – where will stock go? Do you have a separate area to work in?

I have run businesses from home and even small businesses will need a lot of space for stock. The alternative would be to use drop shipping services (where another business stores, dispatches products on your behalf usually for print based businesses) but this can be very costly and leave you with little profit margin.

It is worth mentioning here about personal situations – if you have a family, or a partner at home and you are planning of working from home you need the dedicated space to work from but also to be left alone to work in. This means you can work uninterrupted all day (or however many hours you are choosing to work) and leads me onto another factor needed for space to work – you need to be able to put hours in and not be distracted by tv / phone etc. Which can be a lot harder than you think if you have never worked from home before.

People: If you are starting your business on a budget, it is unlikely you will be able to afford hiring people right away. Even the initial setup may mean you will need to wear many hats and do things yourself in order to save money. Thinking about a website for your business, will you be able to create a fully functioning e-commerce website on your own? Hiring a web developer is expensive but can take the stress away. What about decorating a shop? Every location will need at least some form of decorating as well as fitting out shelves / ways of displaying items.

Along with the initial start-up needed for a business, which people will you need for it to operate? If running the business on your own, you need to factor in personal circumstances such as cover for holidays, or off sick. In life unexpected things happen, so this needs to be factored into your consideration.

Reliance on others can affect your timescales for your business. For example, if you are relying on a printer for a personalised item, you need to make sure delivery times are kept on top of. I suggest a spreadsheet or similar system you can use to track deliveries you will be receiving when buying stock for your business. I do love a good spreadsheet and a list!

Packaging: it may seem simple, but packaging plays an important part of branding. If selling online, you need to factor in costs of what you will be sending your item in. Boxes look great with branded logos but cost a lot more than simple plain packaging. You need to factor full costs ensuring you do not forget anything even down to printing packing slips.

Packaging needs to be bright, engaging and show off your products or services in a way that is instantly recognisable. A simple way to do this would be to have white packaging and buy a stamp with your business logo customised on it. This can look great for food businesses and sort of gives off an expensive look at a low price.

If selling in person, you need to consider bags, packing of your items for customers to take away. If your business is service based, you may not need as much packaging but costs such as flyers, business cards and more.

Packaging can be expensive, be sure to shop around and pay attention to delivery costs. Be sure to consider this with **Place** as to where you will store packaging especially if working from your own home.

Process: this is the transaction – it is the full operation from how a customer places an order to the checkout to pay for goods and how they receive their goods or service. For example, if your business is online via a website you have created: The customer will place an order via your website, full checkout process including placing a debit card payment, as a business owner you will receive the order via the backend of the website and organise shipping the item via a courier. The customer will receive your order (and hopefully be pleased enough to leave a positive review).

You may want to have backups for selling in person (if you use a card machine provider, what if there is not a signal from where you are selling from for example). You will need change (banks will charge you for this) especially if you are selling lots in person. I used to keep a tin of change that I added my own money to and kept for whenever needed.

For me, the best card reader I found for cost is Square. You can use a comparison website to see where has the best deals at the time but I found Square came out on top overall. Consider:

- Price to pay outright for the card reader (or monthly cost of renting which I advise against)
- Price per transaction (usually a couple of percent of the final sale)
- Any charges or extras they will add on

My Square card reader cost around £18 and fees were 2% of the transaction plus 20p.

If you are using selling websites such as Etsy or eBay – consider their charges when setting up.

There is no set way to decide on which business you would like to start as this decision needs to come from you. Many people start businesses from their hobbies if into crafting or making things and form them into a business, which can be easily transferred to selling items on Etsy, local events and more.

Using the seven Ps, writing down your answers to each P will help you begin planning for your business.

What business not to do:

I cannot help you decide on which business is for you. But I will say which business (if you can call them that) not to do and to stay very clear of:

MLMs – known as Multi-Level Marketing. This means companies pay individuals a small percentage of profit on the sales of goods – things like perfumes. MLMs are highly unethical – they encourage people to "recruit" others to join their team and sell products this is done via social media and bothering friends and family. The recruiter (or some sort of stupid made-up title like "managing supervisor of sales") will gain a percentage of their sales and people have the chance to work up higher ranks to gain a better percentage. Exactly like a pyramid scheme. Most of the products MLMs are cheap and they charge extortionate prices for. MLMs will not make any money – the only person getting rich are those at the top of the pyramid.

If you are not sure what an MLM is, I can guarantee you will have seen one on social media (usually Facebook) that people will blindly post similarly stuff from so called companies like:

- FM or Federico Mahora, is one of the biggest MLM's there is. They sell perfume and aftershave fragrances that are "just the same as designer brand names" yet they are not! I tried some testers and they smelt bad, nothing like the brand names.
- Avon
- Bodyshop at home
- Younique
- Usborne Books
- Utility Warehouse

For a full list, see: https://mlmtruth.org/master-list/

Each MLM has shocking pressure sales tactics, shoddy products, and awful practices. Do not support them. Do not even consider starting one – you will lose money.

Let's... Start An Escape Room Business: Step 1- Marketing mix seven Ps:

Product: my product is the escape room itself. I plan to create all puzzles and decorate the room myself to save on money. I will open with one escape room that I run by myself and will expand when business picks up to open other rooms in the same building. There are other escape rooms already established in the area I wish to open but none of those escape rooms have a scary themed room like I plan to open so my room will stand out.

Price: My pricing structure is simple - £20 per person for the full hour minimum of 2 people, with a discount for more players in the same team (up to 6 players per room in total). This compares favourably against the other escape rooms in the area as my pricing is cheaper. I have also compared against other escape rooms further afield and found my pricing is similar or cheaper. I will be open 7 days to begin with, opening from midday to late at night. Slots run every hour and half, giving me 15 minutes to speak to customers when they arrive, go over rules and any questions they may have and brief the team on what they need to do. They will then have 1 hour in the escape room itself and around 5 minutes for a debrief at the end. This leaves me with around 10 minutes to reset the room before the next booking slot.

Place: My chosen location is in a city centre, an old building located near busy bars and restaurants. Parking is an issue, but there are parking spaces nearby with just a ten-minute walk. The space inside is large enough for several escape rooms, a reception area, and toilets for the customers to use. The location is upstairs so will not be accessible for all, which I will need to warn customers about. The noise levels may be an issue, especially late at night with bars playing loud music or noise from different events in the city centre.

People: I plan to create all puzzles for the experience as well as the decorating, I can create a website with a booking system and market the business myself. I will also run the escape room games myself with my partner as a backup if needed. If the business does well, I will consider hiring staff members to run the games. For complex works when building new rooms, I will need electricians / professionals to hire as and when needed. If possible, all works and any tasks would be done by myself or my partner.

Packaging: As the escape room is not a tangible product, there is very little packaging needed. But I plan to purchase certificates for completing the rooms, along with boards to hold for team photos. I will need to purchase flyers and business cards to promote the business.

Process: Customers will book their escape room via my website – this has a live booking system so they can choose how many players, which date and time with updated availability. My website will have a payment provider to take debit / credit card payments. Customers will also be able to book over the phone, in person (cash will be accepted and deposit taken if booking in person for a later date). Gift cards will also be available. Terms and conditions will be listed on the website along with being sent via email when they book.

By now, you must have a business in mind along with how you will sell:

Sell online – such as through your own ecommerce website, or on selling websites such as Etsy or Ebay. You can even sell entirely through social media on a Facebook business page, Tik Tok or Instagram. The same applies if you are wanting to provide a service rather than a product.

Or

Sell In Person – this could be at rented premises, at local events, fairs, or markets. You could even sell from home if you provide a product or service that will not require much space.

A good way to start a business is immediately think of customers and what they buy, what they want / need. If you can come up with a way to sell items they want or need then it will be easier in the long run. Sounds easier said than done, I know but this is the way of thinking you must start if you wish to succeed.

If you already have a business idea in mind, ensure you research into the local area you wish to trade:

is there already a business in the area that provides the same product or service as you?

If so, what are their prices / reviews like? Could you provide something different they do not?

My best advice would be, if you live in a small area – try to start a business that is not already there and there is a need for it. If you live in a larger area or a city, you can still provide a unique service or product if you are creative enough. Try to find a niche, or a way to put a spin on something that already exists.

For example – say if you moved to a small village or area that has lots of residents with dogs, if not there already, why not consider opening a pet shop? A dog grooming salon or similar?

When deciding on a business name, ensure you consider:

What will the customer be searching for? How can I say what the business does in its name?

If you consider naming your business something unusual – this will stand out but does it cover the questions above?

The best way would be to keep it simple, say if you are a plumber maybe go for a name that customers will search for, such as:

Plumber in (area name)

This way, your business name will be a search term! Obviously check what is out there, how you can make your name stand out whilst keeping in mind what customers will be looking for.

Summary: First Step: Where to start

When starting a business, a good way to start is with the Marketing Mix: seven Ps. These are seven different aspects of the business you will need to know the answers for. Your business should be either a gap in the market, or if you offer something more than others currently do.

Consider the Marketing Mix (seven Ps) for your potential business. Write down answers for each of the Ps. Try and write as much as you can, considering each one carefully. The more detailed your answers, the easier it will be to start writing your business plan (more on this later in chapter 4).

Do not – consider an MLM as a business. You will lose money and respect from family and friends! You have been warned.

Step one complete! Just seven more steps to go…

Chapter 2: Step Two – Where Will You Get Your Customers

Where will you get your customers from? Knowing the answer to this is extremely difficult to predict, but it is one of the most overlooked aspects in business. As previously mentioned, if you are considering opening a shop, simply opening the door will not bring floods of people. If you were to do this, you would probably get a few people in (depending on the footfall for the area) but most people will not know your business is there.

On the flip side of this, you may advertise extensively and still get customers not knowing what your business is and where you are. It was always a joy for me to hear "I didn't know you were here" after spending £300 a month on advertising.

If you are looking at selling online, SEO (Search Engine Optimisation – more on this later) will be needed whilst building your website and social media pages. Digital advertising will be key to gaining sales as there are so many different websites, selling pages and social media already established, your business must stand out and good quality digital advertising will drive customers to your website.

Thinking about a recent transaction or purchase you would have done the following:

Considered a product or service that you either need or would like

Researched this product / service (this could be online, in person)

Compared product / price to other websites and shops already available

Proceed to purchase once your decision where to buy from is made

If you can think of this as a customer journey, you need to be able to get your business in front of the customer at each of these steps. You may think it easy, especially if you can generate a lot of traffic (people browsing) to your website, shop or wherever it is you choose to sell from but that is only half the battle. You still need to convince them to purchase and that means being better priced than competitors (or offering an advantage over them if the same price), ensuring the customer is kept happy throughout the process with excellent customer service.

If we take for example this book you are reading, how did you come across it? You will have either googled / searched on amazon for something like:

"Start Up Business Book" or "Books On Starting A Business" or similar. This will then bring up different options for you to consider – then if you came across this book, looked at the book in more detail, maybe you checked the synopsis or reviews and then proceeded to buy through amazon. There could have been other ways you came across it, but this is the bare bones of selling a product as part of where you get your customers from. My customer you, (whom I can only thank!) are part of the market I have aimed this book for – people wanting to start a business and looking for help via a book online.

When deciding which business to start, you will want to choose one that will succeed yet this is near impossible, if you can answer the following questions, it will make it easier to decide where to begin gaining customers:

Who are your customers – this is the most complex research you should undertake, if you can thoroughly understand your potential customers, it will make it easier to sell to them and to succeed. You need to know their age, disposable income, interests and buying habits. The more you know about your customers, advertising and selling to them will be simple.

Where do your customers find out about your business:

You need to know where you will be gaining customers from – you may have a particular market you are aiming your business at and will need to reach them in the most cost-effective way possible. Before opening your business, it would be good to gain either a customer base (if you can build one over social media, or locally) or B2B where you would supply another business, could be contracted or casual basis. Having existing orders or work lined up will help in the long-term.

Some other ways of where customers could find out about your business are:

Digital advertising: this could be paid advertising, such as on Google (paid ads appear at the top of results, along with ad next to them) or Facebook advertising (sponsored posts appearing in user's timelines) and advertising on newspaper / magazine websites with articles.

The most effective ways to advertising are to know your customers, their habits and where they will most likely to buy from.

For my businesses, I have used a mix of both Google advertising and Facebook sponsored post advertising – both have their advantages, but I found Google more successful. It can be difficult to get the balance right in terms of how much money to spend on advertising, you may need to do some of your own testing to see what works best for your business. You could also schedule a video call with a Google advisor for business who can help more with this.

Social Media:

Using social media is the best way to drive customers to your business, even if you do not pay for sponsored posts, you can still reach a large market on Facebook for example. Consider your customer's age and their browsing habits if deciding which social media to use – such as Tik Tok is great for a younger audience, but would not suit advertising a product like mobility aids. Using social media is a great way to engage with your customers directly, you should consider making posts around your expertise and drive customers to purchasing in a fun, friendly and not a pushy way. Using social media to post about products and just to sell to them, often leaves customers uninterested and unwilling to buy. It's a skill to make posts relevant to your business and not just trying to sell all the time.

Decide what tone you would like to use to speak with potential customers – a friendly, professional manner is usually appropriate. You will need to ensure posts are thought out, which dates, times to post and what is popular. Keep on track with new trends too for example, recently Kourtney Kardashian (urgh, I know) held a sign up at a Travis Barker concert to announce she is pregnant. This led to several memes on social media replacing the words on her sign, which cleverly, a lot of big companies picked up on and joined in, posting over Kourtney's sign about their products or services. It is just a bit of fun, evoking a lot of engagement from users but shows that keeping on top of what is popular, works.

To start with, it can feel like a bit like you are posting and getting nothing back, but stick at it. Begin by getting friends and family to like or follow your business over social media and better yet, share your posts. Once you begin to reach the market or accounts that your business is aimed at you will gain a better insight into your customers.

You could try doing a giveaway or competitions to build numbers, these can be great to gain the following you need but people who want something for free, will often enter the competition (let us say you ran it on Facebook as a like / share type) and then unlike / unfollow once the competition is closed. It is a cheap way to advertise – you could give away your product or service so should not cost a lot of money to you, but on the flip side, may not get the quality followers or likes you need, who will buy from you.

There are peak times when to post – such as Facebook peak is 3pm on Friday, possibly due to people leaving work for the end of the week, but other peak times are usually during the evenings or at weekends. Thinking about when you post, is almost as important to as what you post. Posting too little or too often can also have an effect (ensuring customers and people who have liked your page stay engaged).

If you are using Twitter, a post that contains a link is downgraded (and not shown as often on people's feeds) simply add a link in your bio on Twitter – and advise people that is where they can purchase from you.

Threads is the new social media from Facebook / Instagram / Meta at the time of writing I have not had much use of it – from what I can gather, it is like Twitter (hopefully without the right wing hate that the new owner has allowed to run riot) and seems like it is to promote discussions, without hashtags. There are not any advertisers on there currently (apparently Mark Zuckerberg wants a couple of billon accounts signed up before they do monetise it) so it is unclear how companies and business owners will utilise it. It could be a great tool for gaining feedback, having open discussions with customers, potential customers and even suppliers alike.

I have few followers on there so if you would like to follow me on Threads: imamemberofstarsthreads.net

Not everyone will see posts about your business no matter what you do unless you engage with them in some way, but there are tricks to gaining the most views:

- Always post with a picture or a video – posting a line of text will lower the engagement and how it is shown in people's feeds.
- Use hashtags – people can search for certain words / phrases so be sure to research which ones work best and relate to your business or service
- Post once or twice a day at "peak" times – usually in the evening or at weekends

Reviews: on social media can be a big draw for customers – having positive reviews often can be a deciding factor whether to buy, ensure your customers leave reviews and respond accordingly. Bad reviews are annoying but they can also be a way of using experiences as feedback to make your product or service better.

It can be difficult to gain reviews, people are bombarded with them all the time (I often get notifications from Google to review my visit to Sainsbury's for example which is ridiculous) so remind customers in a way that is not too intrusive. I simply asked players in my escape rooms before they left, which seemed to work overall.

I often had custom because people stated they had read reviews and seen that, they were positive and so wanted to see for themselves.

There is a way to pay for fake reviews, which I advise against as they are obvious and often get removed when spotted. Ensure your business is the best it can be and encourage open honest reviews – it will help in the long term.

Word Of Mouth: this is the best (and free) way of advertising – people telling others about your business, product or service can often drive sales. It can be difficult to achieve (you cannot control what people say funnily enough) but if you provide a product or service with excellent service, people take note and will tell others about their positive experience or if they are looking for recommendations. They key to achieving word of mouth is to treat every customer as if they are your last, you want them to return and be happy with what you have done for them. It means going above and beyond their expectations and sometimes this can be easily done, for example if selling products online you could include a gift or treat with their purchase, this could be something as simple as sweets.

Word of mouth Is the cheapest and the most effective form of marketing there is.

Print Advertising: you may think flyers or leaflets are outdated, but they can be a cheap and effective tool in gaining customers. A lot of people will certainly throw flyers in the bin (please consider recycling if you do) but some will read them and even drive them to make a purchase. Print could be in newspapers / magazines to reach a wider market; business cards are great for getting your details out there quickly or in the form of newsletters.

You will need to learn how to write a press release and what constitutes as a good story, or speak with local writers and engage with them directly for them to help you and your business.

Footfall / walk ins: Without combining advertising and using social media, you may get some people walking past if you have a shop, but this depends on footfall in your area. You will get very little business from this method without combining it with another form of marketing.

If you are unsure of the footfall in your area, if you are wanting premises for your business and know where your shop / business will be located, a good way is to find out yourself. Simply sit nearby and watch people each day (if you can all day) from the hours you plan to open and mark down how many people will go past.

It is not an exact science, but you will be able to work out an average number (there will likely be more people at weekends and whenever events are on) and these are all potential customers.

You can even write a profile of ages / sexes of who you see going past.

Or speak to local businesses nearby – you could even see if they will take flyers or any promotional material you may have to help spread the word about your business.

There may be research already available if you are in a BID (Business Improvement District) area or could be online – be sure to check everywhere and gather as much information as you can to help with your business plan.

Let's… Start An Escape Room Business: Step 2 – Where Will You Get Customers From

For my escape room business, I will use a mix of social media (Facebook, Instagram, and Twitter, using competitions or giveaways to gain likes and drive engagement) some flyers for local businesses and residents to gain 10% off their booking and I will contact the local newspaper with a story based on the escape room itself.

Using social media, I will keep customers engaged with my pages by discussing escape rooms, their ideas for new rooms and keep it light hearted with memes, jokes, and general light banter.

I plan to use Google advertising once launched to continue gaining bookings – initially starting low and increasing as the business develops. Estimate is around £100-£300 per month.

Summary: Step 2 – Where Will You Get Customers From

Gaining customers will require a lot of thought for your own business or service. This will be entirely your choice; ensure you use the best techniques or a mixture to gain attention. You could do an initial launch party, invite the local press, or keep it low key with exclusive offers to entice people.

Whatever you choose to do for your business, ensure you open and do something, rather than doing nothing and getting nowhere. You need to remember gaining customers is an ongoing issue you need to solve rather than just at launch.

Chapter 3: Step 3 – Marketing Your Business

Marketing your business will seem like where you get your customers from as it will involve advertising your business, but it is also how you brand your business in general from how you speak with customers (such as tone of voice). Building a strong brand ensures customers can recognise your business instantly, even if they are new customers, your branding should tell customers who you are and what your business does.

Branding: this does not mean to just slap a logo on t shirts, branding is so much more and something you should be doing throughout your day as a business owner. If you have certain colours and fonts, these should be used throughout your business from the logo, to social media banners and even printed flyers, notes and more. This is known as having a uniform for your business (they must be recognisable, if you think of huge brands like Coca Cola, their colours of a red and white logo spring to mind right away) and a big part of branding.

Your tone when used to speak with customers is a part of branding. When you pick up the phone, you should be saying your business name, signing emails off with your business signature and so on. On social media, try to keep light hearted but still professional. For example, responding to a post from a customer who is complaining will not appreciate a humorous style of writing.

Social Media: This has been mentioned a lot already, you should have already setup business pages on social media sites like Facebook, Instagram, Tik Tok etc. Ensure when you do, as part of branding, that each username is the same or as near as possible to your business. For example, I would brand my escape room business as @LetsStartAnEscapeRoom across all social media, if for whatever that username is taken, I would consider changing all social media to @LetUsStartAnEscapeRoom and so on until each page has the same name.

Be sure to use hashtags relevant to your business, keep up to date with notable days in the calendar – not just the holidays such as Easter, Christmas, Eid etc but also days centred around products. For example:
-    National chocolate eating day
-    Wine drinking day
-    Coffee Day

I am sure you get the idea. A good way of keeping up to date with these marketable events is to plan, use a calendar and publish posts automatically ahead of time. There are applications / websites you can use to help schedule posts in advance across all platforms like Hoot Suite / Tweet Deck but I have not any experience using these. I did used to schedule posts on Facebook whenever I was away. You need to keep followers engaged, so if you do not post regularly, fewer, and fewer people will see the posts you do.

Along with posting on your own social media pages, try and gain likes or followers via local selling pages or pages around your product or niche. Research beforehand which are the most relevant pages to your business and have the biggest following. Bear in mind, that each local page or group will have their own specific rules about posting as a business. It is a good and free way of gaining some exposure and hopefully if you post the correct content, some new likes, and followers to your business page but bear in mind group rules – some are funny about businesses posting or allow only certain times / days for when businesses can post.

You need to find ways of firstly, standing out from your business competition and then marketing this to potential customers. This in turn will drive customers to make a purchase or use your service.

Marketing campaigns:

A marketing campaign is an idea put into practice to either promote your business or to achieve a specific business goal (such as gaining a certain number of followers on social media).

You will need to use several marketing campaigns throughout owning a business and it can be a simple plan of how you will reach your goals, it does not have to be as complicated as it sounds.

Marketing campaigns will usually cost (such as paid advertising) but some can be free if you are creative enough to gain exposure. This could be through a press release and a local newspaper may pick up the story – giving your business exposure.

Marketing Ideas

Countdown to launch date

Do not wait until your business is live before you start your marketing activities. Build awareness of your business before it is published and get people excited about the launch day. You could offer exclusive discounts on pre-release orders, or send out sneak previews of the products available, or post short snippets in the days leading up to the launch date.

Landing page

If you are selling your business or service through your own website, set up a dedicated landing page that tells people why they should buy from your business. You can then link to this from your blog, guest blogs and email footer. You could have an offer or a discount that pops up for visiting your website.

You might even want to run pay per click ads that link to your landing page if the topic is something people are likely to be searching.

Blog post

Create a blog post or a series of blog posts about your business explaining why you have started it and who it is for. Let people know about your business or service; get them invested in it.

If you write guest posts, then make sure you mention your business. Suggest ideas for guest posts that tie in with your business. Utilise your business network and look for opportunities to tap into a wider audience.

Do not bombard your audience with sales posts; show them why your business will be a good investment.

Email footer

Include a link to your business in your email footer or signature. That could be a link to your landing page, to a blog post about your sales page. Every time you email someone, you will be promoting your business.

Launch event

If you have the budget, you could host a launch event where you can talk about your business and sell some products. Invite those who helped make the business possible, your clients and potential clients as well as any local media or companies who would be interested in promoting the business for you.

Interviews

Find radio, TV, magazines, or newspapers that are running stories that could be tied into your industry. Offer your services as a subject expert in return for a chance to promote your business. For example, if your business is about accountancy for small businesses, you could be interviewed about any upcoming changes that are being made to tax liabilities.

Networking events & exhibitions

Find local networking events where you can promote your business, or take a stand at an exhibition where you can sell or give away samples. Ask about speaking opportunities at events, conferences and seminars and put together a talk that ties in with your business. If suitable offer a service to a school – as kids will talk / remember about your business.

Influencers

Research influencers in your industry and ask them to help promote your business. You could send them a free product, reference them in your business bio where appropriate, or utilise paid promotion opportunities. I have never used an influencer before so I am not too sure how well this would work.

Google My Business

This is an absolute must for all businesses. You need a Google profile to set up Google My Business. We all use Google; it has become the main search engine for everybody and will be the first-place customers will look to find your business – they may come across it through:

- Google search – this could bring up your website if you have optimised your website correctly (see further down more about SEO – Search Engine Optimisation) it may bring up certain parts on a specific page depending on what the user is searching for. Let us use the search term: Escape Rooms London. This will bring up several escape room businesses located in and around London (if they have done their SEO correctly) it could bring up their homepage or landing page or even to the booking section of their site
- Google Maps – this is if you have a physical location or premises for customers to come visit. Ensure details are correct (such as contact number as well as address)
- Product suggestions – these are suggestions of products that match your search. Say if you were looking for a new Air fryer, you will search for it on google and pictures of air fryers along with prices and where is selling them will show on the top of the google search result.
- Sponsored posts at the top of search results – these are posts that companies pay google to show. It could show a brief description that relates to your search, will often include a link.

If you are setting up Google My business you will need to request to google that your details for a location (they will send a postcard in the post to verify your address details) and update with details of your business.

The more information you give to Google, the better.

Google even have product suggestions on your business posts – which can take time to fill out but if your customers come across your Google profile, they can then see products, potentially leading to a sale.

Even if you do not use Google my business (and you should!) Google will index your website if you have one, via spiders. These are what crawl across the internet to gather data about your website and your business.

SEO – Search Engine Optimisation

This is not as scary as it sounds and will do a lot of the hard work for you if your business relies on traffic to your website. Search Engine Optimisation means to design your website in a way that Google will favour.

It means each page on your website needs to have a meta description (what is shown on the links of your website on Google), Key words or phrases that relate to your business and products you sell that people might search for.

Any images should have meta and alt text descriptions (include your business name as much as you can) and your website should be formatted for both mobile and desktop browsers.

Try to keep your website loading speed under 2 seconds. This is so Google will favour your website. You can check your website speed via a checker, most are free to use and can even help show where you can save time.

Link all pages in your website, ensuring no dead links and try to get other websites to backlink to yours. A backlink is where an established website or blog will link to your business from their website. It can be really beneficial in the long term, to gain traffic (people) to your website and Google will rank your site higher on search results.

Google will favour websites with contact details on the header or footer (I am not sure why) and websites that are clear what the business is or what the business offers in terms of products or services.

SEO is easy to do yourself (especially with websites like Wix) but you can hire SEO experts to do it for you. I suggest having a go and looking up any YouTube videos or help articles if you are still unsure.

Blogging

An easy way to get key words in, blogs can go into detail about your business and products. It needs to be entertaining for people to want to read but getting in key phrases will help overall. Blogging around your business or products could be like the following subjects (I will use escape rooms as an example):

- Top 10 tips to complete and escape room
- Best escape rooms in your area
- Escape Rooms for beginners

And so on – the top 10 idea seems to work great for most businesses, just be sure to include links to your products and mention key words and phrases that your customers will use to find your business.

How not to market your business:

Not all news coverage is good news and while I would say give everything and anything a go to promote your business, there are a few things you should not do:

Do not use Groupon / Wowcher other social buying websites or apps

Do not use Groupon, Wowcher or any other similar website as it will devalue your business.

I decided to use Groupon and Wowcher during the pandemic to promote online escape games I had built. Yes, it did get me a lot of customers (and I do not like to speak bad of customers but from Groupon almost all of them were dissatisfied with everything) but Groupon wanted me to discount my games (which were already low cost as it is) massively – and they would take a 30% portion of that sale on top.

It was not worth doing – I asked for the games I were offering to be automated service which Groupon refused to do – meaning after I had signed a contract with them offering my games at a low price, I also had to send games out to every single customer whenever purchased. This meant me sending emails out to every single customer with their game and it was all day and night. People would buy the Groupon and want to play the games right away (which is fine as I would probably want to do the same) but because Groupon did not automate this as a service – I would get emails and calls late at night (some even at midnight) from Groupon customers wanting their game.

I had a better experience with Wowcher but I still had a similar problem with the automated service.

I know these are my experiences and you could benefit from using Groupon, I would suggest otherwise.

If you want to gain customers, simply budget an amount, and use Google advertising to gain customers. Sure, you are either spending or gaining a small percentage of a sale if you decide to use Groupon but the difference Is – you set your pricing and stick to it and keep all the profit.

An example of Groupon being bad for business, I have seen offers for escape rooms with Groupon – great for customers but bad for the business. If their pricing for an escape room is £80 for 5 or 6 people, Groupon would run a campaign for at least 50% off that price. So, if it is a Groupon offer at £40 for a group of 5 or 6 – the escape room is getting £40 less 30% for Groupon to take (sometimes it can be more, they did try to charge me a higher percentage) at £12 = £28 profit for the escape room. But also take into consideration business bills, paying staff members, insurance, etc it leaves very little!

Using Groupon will devalue your business – if you ran a campaign with them for 6 months at one price and after this at another price, customers will be unhappy paying more if they have had it for less.

I know this is true for all businesses with discounts and sales, customers will be charged for the same item differently – but with Groupon mainly being for businesses that specialise in things for customers to do, it leaves no profit, which is pointless really.

Let's Start An Escape Room: Step 3 – Marketing Your Business

Summary: Step 3 – Marketing Your Business

Ensure you have clear branding for your business, including uniform colours, fonts, and tone. Setup all social media pages with the same name (such as @YourBusinessName) this should be the same for email addresses as well as social media.

Start planning marketing campaigns based around your business goals, these could be short term and long-term goals. Ensure you market your business on Google, social media and in any way you can think of to promote it except for using websites like Groupon. Avoid them!

Chapter 4: Step 4 – Writing A Business Plan

This next section will be the actual business plan I used to start my escape room business. I changed the name to Let's Start An Escape Room Business for the purpose of this book and have not given details of where it was actually located (I refer to the location as The City as it was city centre based) because I sold the business and it is still open. There is a blank business plan template for you to use here:

https://tinyurl.com/BusBlank

Filling in your business plan with as much detail as you can will help your business in the long term and may help with financing (if looking for a loan to get started) or other funding.

What is a business plan?

A business plan is a formal document that indicates what your business idea is, sort of putting to paper your concept or service you intend to do. It usually consists of detailed descriptions of your business, where it will be located, the market and customer base along with cashflows and financials.

It can be daunting to write a long document (I found that the financials were not my strong suit) about a business if you are still in the planning stages, my blank template and example should help with this.

Why is a business plan needed?

A business plan can help you with planning your business, it is an essential asset to keep you on track, help with finances and will be needed if you are planning to apply for a loan.

It is a good tool to use (and keep updated) for long term and short-term goals, even past when you have launched the business. If you think of it like a diary for your business thoughts, it will be something you add to regularly.

Your plan can keep you motivated, help guide you if stuck and will help your business in general.

If applying for grants, loans, or any other financial help, you will need to use your business plan to apply for them.

Business Plan – Filled In real example

1. Executive summary and description

- **The product/service:**

    Let's Start An Escape Room Business is an escape room, where customers are "locked" into a room with clues and puzzles to solve in order to escape within a time limit. There will be initially 2 rooms to open with, each with a different theme – which are:

    - **Room 1:** <u>Scary Escape Room:</u> An evil cursed item has locked you and your friends within a scary haunted place – with only 60 minutes on the clock, will you be able to escape before play time is over?
    - **Room 2:** <u>Exploring Escape Room:</u> An Egyptian god was tricked into laying in a golden coffin, that was sealed and cut into pieces, lost throughout Egypt. Osiris needs your help to find the pieces to enable his soul to rest in peace – within the time limit of 60 minutes.

    There will be further rooms opening as the business expands, investing profit into other rooms and improving on the ones already open with revamps of puzzles and décor as needed.

- ### The customer profile:

The business will be in the city centre. Customers will primarily be aged 18-50 with disposable income each week of around £50+. Customers will be made up of friends, families, and work colleagues.

Customers will benefit from a pricing structure that is cheaper for more people playing in a team – based on 5 people per team at £17 each – total £85 per game. Aiming to serve 20 teams per week.

Customers will benefit from loyalty discount codes as well as special themed nights – aiming to maximise profit and making the business stand out from already established escape rooms.

- ### The owner/s of the company:

Matthew James is the owner for the company a young entrepreneur who has previously managed and owned an American sweet shop. Before this, he managed a very busy and successful American sweet store in Sheffield City centre identifying a gap in the market in his own home seaside town. He set to work, researching, and writing a thorough business plan for a store. Then, after renovating a derelict store to a very high standard on a tight budget, he launched the store to much success with some controversy from locals, however the store expanded quickly – different product ranges added each week. He has also studied Sales Management and Marketing approved by the ISMM and became a sales manager for a busy and reputable health and safety company.

The sweet shop was launched with minimal funding and opened for 6 months, to minimise any risk associated with starting a business and to cash in on the busy seasonal period (The seaside is usually busiest during summer which helped make it a success). Social media campaigns were key to making the business a success with over 1,000 likes on Facebook, with a 5-star rating.

- **The expected achievements of the business in the first year of trading:**

1. Thoroughly research, plan and complete business plans for Let's Start An Escape Room
2. To successfully secure funding for the business – applying for grants as match funding
3. Renovate and fit out a unit to a high standard within budget allowances
4. Launch website and social media campaigns to support the marketing of the business
5. Launch the business with build up from social media campaigns and marketing campaigns
6. Work with local businesses, to cross promote, with unique offers.
7. Maintain at least 20 bookings per week – increasing to 25 when new rooms open

- **The future of the company:**

8. Expand the business, investing profits into new rooms
9. Expand existing rooms / hire more staff as required
10. Sell to different markets – such as offices for work away days, weddings, events etc
11. Launch different themed nights
12. Expand into a different area, opening a second unit

- **The most important strengths and competencies of the company:**

Unique brand and concept as a business idea. The itself will benefit from the owner previously working at a local escape room business.

Pricing is key to making the business a success, Let's Start An Escape Room's pricing is very competitive in comparison to existing escape rooms in the local area – often being much cheaper, more valuable for money.

2. Unique selling point (USP)

The concept for Let's Start An Escape Room Business (no other escape rooms have the same theme). Unique Selling Points (USPs) include:

- Unique pricing structure
- Competitively priced in comparison to other escape rooms
- Customer focused on providing excellent customer service and unique experiences
- Excellent knowledge of existing rooms, prices, and availability
- Very low ongoing running costs after initial investment
- Unique puzzles, experiences not seen in other escape rooms in the area with a scary theme being unique
- Spend time with customers who want to chat – building relationships

3. Career history

Experience:

Date	Company	Location (city)	Job title	Skills gained

Qualifications:
(Vocational, non-vocational)

Date	Organisation	Location	Course	Qualification/s

Reason for career change:

After having been self-employed previously, I am fully aware of the stress, challenges and strain put under whilst self-employed. However, I have learnt a lot of lessons from previously being self-employed and feel I have more determination, desire, and drive to succeed in business with this.

After working for another employer now feels strange and uninspiring. I miss the buzz of earning sales for myself and moving the business forward in ways that I want to. I enjoy working hard, putting in time, energy, and effort to achieve the best results.

4. About my service/product

Let's Start An Escape Room Business is a unique escape room concept, with unique themes and original puzzles not seen anywhere else nearby. The business will launch initially with one room, then expand with different themes for new rooms. It will also benefit from a yearly pop-up Christmas themed escape room that changes each year.

Prices for players are as follows:

- Team of 2 = £40 (£20pp)
- Team of 3 = £57 (£19pp)
- Team of 4 = £72 (£18pp)
- Team of 5 = £85 (£17pp)
- Team of 6 = £96 (£16pp)

To ensure sales targets are met, need to gain **20+ bookings per week**.

Discounts are available for larger teams if booking several rooms at the same time. There will be a 10% off code widely available at launch, to encourage bookings initially.

5. Aims, objectives, employment

Personal aims and objectives:

1. Save **£3,000** as part of start-up costs (estimated £5,000 needed In total)
2. Ensure kept up to date with marketing trends and selling techniques
3. Train in first aid

Business aims and objectives:

1. Thoroughly research into the business idea and the target city
2. Secure funding for the business (applied for **£2,000** from City Council) raise **£3,000** from savings
3. Build upon social media pages Facebook, Twitter, Instagram
4. Renovate a room to a high standard, remaining in costs and budget
5. Design and launch information website with booking system
6. Launch business with build up from social media campaigns and marketing campaign
7. Launch loyalty scheme
8. Ensure booking at least 20 teams per week
9. Launch new rooms
10. Expand into different markets – such as weddings, celebrations / events

Key people (responsibilities):

Sales & Marketing:	Matthew James
Operations:	Matthew James
Financial management:	Matthew James

I aim to provide employment eventually, once Let's Start An Escape Room has established a reputation and gaining a regular income. I will require part time employees who would suit working with their own commitments. I aim to give unemployed or people in need of training a chance to gain vital skills, in customer service, and sales when expanded.

My ethos is to be a social hub for the community looking to support other businesses, & involve the local community as much as I can. This could be, by being actively involved in local events, sponsoring local teams or being involved in any way.

I have been in contact with a local magazine named Browse, who is working with us to run a feature spread upon opening – we will be stocking the magazine in return, free to customers to read / take away. Potential for advertorials and to reach target market.

6. Legal Matters

Premises:

Premises will be in the city – ideally will be either near local shops and bars. The unit will be subject to permission obtained from City Council (For change of business use).

The unit itself will need to be in good condition, have enough space for at least several escape rooms and area for customers / somewhere private to watch games and help players. It will need toilets and be accessible.

Potential unit in the city with 3 floors – so lots of space for potential escape rooms.

State any licenses/registrations/insurances that are needed for your business:

A change of use for the business class is required from the City Council before opening.

General business insurance will be needed (from simplybusiness.co.uk) and public liability insurance for up to £5m.

Fire Precautions:

Let's Start An Escape Room Business will:
- Carry out a fire risk assessment of the premises and review it regularly, keeping accurate records
- Tell staff or their representatives, customers and all visitors about the risks identified
- Put in place, and maintain, appropriate fire safety measures
- Plan for an emergency evacuation – include signage in all escape rooms
- Provide staff information, fire safety instruction and training
- Extinguishers, alarms, and fire certificates will be obtained from the local fire brigade or online

Health and Safety Regulations:

All Health and Safety Regulations will be complied with as per instructions from the HSE website. (www.hse.gov.uk)This will include all fire safety, first aid and systems in place to ensure a safe environment. All HSE approved signage in all the correct locations.

Data Protection Act

Customer's personal details such as email address and telephone numbers will be collated via an "opt in" option either via newsletter on the website or by entering competitions this will be kept on a secure server and only contacted as per customer requests. This will be kept on a secure server for up to 3 years.

As customer details are needed to secure booking and make a payment, they can opt out of any marketing with a tick box on the website during the checkout process.

7. Suppliers

Who will be your major suppliers?

Let's Start An Escape Room will be independent business and most works will be carried out by Matthew James. Suppliers will be:

- Locks needed from whichever website is cheapest with the best availability
- Electronic and props from Escape Room Suppliers / made by Matthew James
- A lot of decorating equipment for initial set-up (paints etc) from B&Q

8. The market place

Market Size

Let's Start An Escape Room Business will be based in the busy shopping / bar area of City – a popular retail avenue with a variety of bars, restaurants, and shops. It is a busy, thriving area and is being regenerated recently.

There are 2 other escape rooms in the local area, one independent and one chain business. Their prices compare as follows:

Escape Room Chain business:

2 People £22 3 People £21 4 People £19
5 People £17 6 People £16

Independent Escape Room:

2 People £25 3 People £23 4 People £20 5 People £18
6 People £16.50

Market research information obtained from the internet/reference books

1. The market is still growing
Since the first escape room opened doors in 2007, the industry has grown to reach people from all over the world. According to recent data, there are over 3,000 escape games in Europe and around 14,000 worldwide.

And while nothing goes up in a straight line forever, the escape room market is still on the rise. According to the State of the Escape Room Industry Report 2018, 59% of escape room owners reported having plans to expand within the next year.

Also, almost 7 in 10 respondents (68.33%) said that they will add at least one more room to their current location. This not only indicates that many owners feel that the popularity of Escape Rooms continues to rise but also shows that the supply has yet to overwhelm the demand.

The industry is still very profitable and entrepreneurs report that the cost of launching their first venue pays off within a year.

2. Higher competition
Escape games took off but the market is getting more stabilized and mature rather than growing exponentially. We all know how every flourishing industry attracts several entrepreneurs to invest in. Escape rooms are not an exception.

In some cities, especially capitals, the number of rooms is getting very high, which makes this market more and more competitive. In general, it is now more difficult to launch new ones, but also to grow and maintain existing games.

The competition is rising and so are people's expectations. The July 2018 Escape Room Industry Growth Study finds a substantial increase in the number of room closures in the UK last year.

For some keywords such as Escape game + name of your city, you probably saw a cost increase compared to 2-3 years ago.

New call-to-action
3. Saturated Market
The traditional escape game is no longer a novelty and everyone requires high-quality sets, props, and technology. People want a real challenge and an engaging experience like no other. Below are some ideas that will help you differentiate in a saturated market.

New Channel Development:
The Escape game industry was the victim of its success. The concept was trendy, everyone wanted to try it and everyone was talking about it. Therefore, Escape room owners stayed in their comfort zone and focused on only one channel – B2C.

To be more precise, the main and unique revenue stream for some of the providers was direct end-consumer sales with a strong online share.

However, given the maturity of the market and the reduced "new-trend" effect, it's required to innovate also commercially speaking and develop new channels like Business-to-Business (team building, corporate retreats, etc.).

B2B can also be online thanks to all e-commerce marketplaces dedicated to leisure activities and new ones even specialized in Escape games.

Movie-inspired escape rooms:
More and more theme inspired rooms open, all of them providing innovative activities aimed at particular audiences.

From Harry Potter, Lost and Prison Break, to Breaking Bad and Game of Thrones, escape rooms take the excitement to the next level by letting ordinary people experience the characters' challenge first hand.

Creating a movie-inspired room seems to be a great way to be different and guarantees a high level of engagement. By giving a new life to some of the all-time favorite stories and characters you can accommodate a large subset of customers.

According to The Top Escape Rooms Project, researching escape games all over the world, most of the successful venues are inspired by some horror movie motives.

4. Big focus on safety
We see more and more escape rooms prioritizing health and safety to prevent accidents and comply with government regulations.

5. Increasing reliance on online bookings
Offering the most unique experience out there is not enough. The 2018 Escape Room Industry Report found abundant evidence indicating the crucial impact of an escape room's website.

Major competitors

There are 2 other escape room companies in the local area.

One is a chain, with many other escape rooms throughout the UK. This escape room has 5 different themed escape rooms and employs around 4 members of staff.

The other is an independent escape room with 4 different themed escape games.

Their prices are:

Escape Room Chain business:

2 People £22   3 People £21 4 People £19 5 People £17 6 People £16

Independent Escape Room:

2 People £25   3 People £23 4 People £20 5 People £18 6 People £16.50

UK wide escape room companies with many different branches include:

Escape
Breakout
Cluequest
Enigma

New or other products or services you intend to sell later

Initially, there will be just the one escape room to launch the business with. This is so there is a quick turnaround from setup to opening and to ensure small budget is adhered to.

Eventually, Let's Start An Escape Room will have 4 escape rooms, along with a Christmas themed pop up escape room which changes each year.

With potential to offer merchandise or printed photos as part the experience.

Could work with other local businesses to offer packages such as escape rooms and drinks or food all for one price.

9. Business Operations

Where will you be located?

The store will be located in the City benefitting from a parade of popular shops and bars with a coffee culture feel. This will ensure maximum bookings as people will benefit booking the escape rooms, being able to shop or go out for dinner either before or after.

How will your product be made and distributed (for product-based businesses) or how will you serve your customers?

Customers will be able to book in online via – staff will consist of me (Matthew James) to begin with, leading to more staff (on a part time basis to suit both business and their needs) as sales grow.

In Month 12, at least 2 escape rooms will be up and running along with the pop-up Christmas escape game.

How do you receive products/services from your suppliers?

This is not needed other than the initial setup. Suppliers can deliver to door at the business location.

What quality-control measures will you implement, if any?

The escape rooms will be cleaned thoroughly between games – this includes using antibacterial wipes to clean all surfaces, locks and wherever players will have been able to touch.

PAT tests will be conducted on all electrical items with a socket.

Fire alarm tests and records will be kept, ensuring all teams are aware of the fire escape plan if it were to occur during their escape room game.

How will you measure customer satisfaction?

Customer satisfaction will be measured via Face book ratings (star rating out of 5) and other social media platforms to monitor closely what customers would like to see in the escape rooms (in terms of popularity, new rooms etc). Satisfaction will also be measured via Trip Advisor reviews – to see what customers opinions are of the escape room business. Customers will be encouraged to rate / write reviews.

How and when will you keep you books and monitor business performance?

Books and records will be kept daily from sales performance to invoices / receipts etc. Business performance will be measured using a system similar to Covalent to measure month on month growth and to stress test any impacts on the business (such as busy periods etc)

10. Sales & marketing plan - estimates, advertising, and sales methods:

a) Advertising and promotion

1. Leaflets / flyers	Monthly	£ 20
2. Online advertising	Monthly	£ 20
3. Social Media advertising	Monthly	£ 60

b) What prices will be charged for the products/services:

Product/Service	Sales Price
Escape room for 2 people	£40.00
Average price	£ 40.00 (AOV)

c) Your sales methods (tick as necessary)

☒ Leaflet drops
☐ Brochure/leaflet mailers
☐ newspaper / magazine advertising
☐ Voucher/Birthday Cards
☒ Email
☐ Events
☐ Exhibitions
☐ Roadside banners

☐ Reseller
☐ Retail store/s
☐ Distributor / wholesaler
☐ Cold call (telephone)
☐ Door to door
☒ Website (online transactions)
☐ Referral/ word of mouth
☒ Other (specify)

(other) Via social media – such as Face Book sponsored posts or Google Advertising etc

11. What if?

What are the effects on your plan if actual sales were 20% less than your forecast?

If sales were 20% less than forecast, this would result in profit down to just break even. This can be combated through ensuring each customer's Average Order Value (AOV) is above £40 (asking for in the future for upgrades such as printed team photos) highlighting new rooms coming or gift vouchers.

If sales were lower, more work would be needed to promote the escape rooms and business. This could be through incentives like discounting rooms or offering competitions such as being able to win back the price of a game if booked at certain days and times.

As I will be living in my partner in the city, he has agreed to support me financially if needed so can reduce my outgoings as a backup.

How would you cope if sales were 20% more than your forecast?

If sales were 20% more than forecasted, the business plan will have to be adjusted – for the other escape rooms and materials, hire more staff if needed and adjusting each area.

How will you plan to run your business in the event of sickness or injury to yourself or any key personnel?

The business will be run by other staff members in the event of sickness or injury to me. Or in the worst-case scenario, my partner will help with the business if needed.

12. Survival income analysis

How much do you need to live on?	Monthly	Yearly
Mortgage or rent	£ 350	£ 4,200
Council tax	£ 0	£ 0
Water rates, sewerage	£ 0	£ 0
Gas/Oil/Coal/Calor Gas	£ 0	£ 0
Electricity	£ 0	£ 0
Telephone	£ 12	£ 144
House insurance	£ 0	£ 0
Contents insurance	£ 0	£ 0
Life assurance	£ 0	£ 0
Pension	£ 30	£ 360
Housekeeping • food, cleaning.	£150	£ 1800
Clothes	£ 50	£ 600
Vehicle Costs - if not charged to business		
Road fund tax	£ 0	£ 0
Insurance	£ 0	£ 0
Repairs and renewals	£ 0	£ 0
MOT	£ 0	£ 0
Fuel	£ 0	£ 0
Travel expenses	£ 50	£ 600

Holidays and trips out	£ 50	£ 600
TV license	£ 0	£ 0
Newspapers and magazines	£ 0	£ 0
Entertainment, meals out, smoking	£ 100	£ 1200
Subscriptions	£ 0	£ 0
Children's pocket money, school trips and	£ 0	£ 0

schools dinners		
Presents for birthdays, Christmas etc	£ 50	£ 600
Hire purchase payments	£ 0	£ 0
Credit or charge cards	£ 150	£ 1800
Allowance for things needing replacement	£ 0	£ 00
Allowance for things needing repair	£ 0	£ 0
Repairs to house	£ 0	£ 0
Contingencies	£ 50	£ 600
SUB TOTAL (A)	£ 1042	£ 12504
Less other household incomes		
Partner's income	£ 0	£ 0
Insurance	£ 0	£ 0
Child allowance	£ 0	£ 0
Maintenance	£ 0	£ 0
Interest and dividends	£ 0	£ 0
SUB TOTAL (B)	£ 1042	£ 12504
TOTAL (C=A-B)	£ 1042	£ 12504

Take the monthly total (c) and enter this amount into the drawings line on the Cashflow chart each month.

13. Business overheads

How much will your business spend be?	Monthly	Yearly
Business property rent and business rates	£ 625	£7500
Business property light, heat, and power (e.g. electricity)	£ 100	£1200
Depreciation *	£ N/A	£ N/A
Employees' wages and employer's national insurance	£ 1000	£ 12000
Finance charges (e.g. bank charges and interest)**	£ 0	£ 0
Insurance costs	£ 100	£1200
Motor expenses (tax, fuel, maintenance)	£ 0	£ 0
Other travelling expenses	£ 0	£ 0
Post and carriage	£ 0	£ 0
Printing and stationery	£ 10	£ 120
Professional fees - e.g. solicitors and accountants	£ 100	£ 1200
Repairs and maintenance	£ 100	£ 1200
Telephone	£ 40	£ 480
Advertising	£ 100	£ 1200
Consumables (e.g. replacing small tools)	£ 0	£ 0
Other expenses	£ 0	£ 0
TOTAL	£ 2,175	£ 26,100

14. Start-up cost e.g. machinery, premises, stationery etc.

1. Room 1	£ 1,600	Website	£ 100
2. Room 2	£ 1,600	Signage	£ 500
3. Spare locks / supplies	£ 100	Online Advertising	£ 200
4. Legal costs	£ 400	Decoration / paint	£ 200
5. H&S	£ 200	Business cards/flyers	£ 100

15. Funding required to start-up

1. Bank

£ 0

2. Owner/self

£ 3,000

3. Grants and other sources

£2,000

Total: £ 5,000

16. Cash flow forecast

Year 1	Month 1	Month 2	Month 3	Month 4	Month 5	Month 6	Month 7	Month 8	Month 9	Month 10	Month 11	Month 12	TOTAL
Capital (Cash) Introduced	5,000												5,000
SALES/ INCOME													
Sales Room 1	1,672	2,000	2,100	2,100	2,100	2,200	2,200	2,200	2,200	2,200	2,200	2,200	25,372
Sales Room 2	1,672	2,000	2,100	2,100	2,100	2,200	2,200	2,200	2,200	2,200	2,200	2,200	25,372
Sales Room 3	0	0	0	1,000	1,000	1,100	1,100	1,100	1,200	1,200	1,200	1,200	10,100
Total Sales	3,344	4,000	4,200	5,200	5,200	5,500	5,500	5,500	5,600	5,600	5,600	5,600	60,844
TOTAL INCOME	8,344	4,000	4,200	5,200	5,200	5,500	5,500	5,500	5,600	5,600	5,600	5,600	65,844
Direct Cost A	0	0	0	0	0	0	0	0	0	0	0	0	0
Direct Cost B	0	0	0	0	0	0	0	0	0	0	0	0	0
Direct Cost C	0	0	0	0	0	0	0	0	0	0	0	0	0
Stock/ Materials	0	100	100	100	100	100	100	100	100	100	100	100	1,100
TOTAL AVAILABLE COST	0	100	100	100	100	100	100	100	100	100	100	100	1,100
Rent/ Rates	625	625	625	625	625	625	625	625	625	625	625	625	7,500
Light/ Heat/ Water	100	100	100	100	100	100	100	100	100	100	100	100	1,200
Fixed Wages & Salaries	1,000	1,000	1,000	1,000	1,000	2,000	2,000	2,000	2,000	2,000	2,000	2,000	19,000
Loan Repayments	0	0	0	0	0	0	0	0	0	0	0	0	0
Insurance costs	100	100	100	100	100	100	100	100	100	100	100	100	1,200
Motor expenses	0	0	0	0	0	0	0	0	0	0	0	0	0
Petrol/ Diesel	0	0	0	0	0	0	0	0	0	0	0	0	0
Professional fees	0	0	0	0	0	0	0	0	0	0	0	0	0
Capital Equipment	0	0	0	0	0	0	0	0	0	0	0	0	0
Telephone	40	40	40	40	40	40	40	40	40	40	40	40	480
Marketing & Promotion	100	100	100	100	100	100	100	100	100	100	100	100	1,200
Consumables	25	25	25	25	25	25	25	25	25	25	25	25	300
Post and carriage	0	0	0	0	0	0	0	0	0	0	0	0	0
Printing and stationery	10	10	10	10	10	10	10	10	10	10	10	10	120
Contingencies	40	40	40	40	40	40	40	40	40	40	40	40	480
Other	0	0	0	0	0	0	0	0	0	0	0	0	0
Other	0	0	0	0	0	0	0	0	0	0	0	0	0
TOTAL FIXED COSTS	2,040	2,040	2,040	2,040	2,040	3,040	3,040	3,040	3,040	3,040	3,040	3,040	31,480
Drawings	0	0	0	0	0	0	0	0	0	0	0	0	0
START UP COSTS	5,000	0	0	0	0	0	0	0	0	0	0	0	5,000
TOTAL SPENDING	7,040	2,140	2,140	3,240	3,240	3,140	3,140	3,140	3,140	3,140	3,140	3,140	39,180
OPENING CASH	0	1,304	3,164	5,224	6,884	9,744	12,104	14,464	16,824	19,284	21,744	24,204	0
TOTAL INCOME	8,344	4,000	4,200	5,200	5,200	5,500	5,500	5,500	5,600	5,600	5,600	5,600	65,844
TOTAL SPENDING	7,040	2,140	2,140	3,740	3,740	3,140	3,140	3,140	3,140	3,140	3,140	3,140	51,480
NET CASH FLOW	1,304	1,860	2,060	1,460	1,460	2,360	2,360	2,360	2,460	2,460	2,460	2,460	
CLOSING CASH	1,304	3,164	5,224	6,884	9,744	12,104	14,464	16,824	19,284	21,744	24,204	26,664	

17. Profit and loss forecast (per year)

Sales forecast (per yr)		**£** **65,844**	
Less: Stock/ materials (per yr)		**£** **2,700**	
Gross profit (per yr)		**£** **63,144**	**Calculation:** (Sales forecast minus stock/materials)
Overheads (per yr)			
Business rent & rates	£ 7,500		
Heat, light & power	£ 1,200		
Fixed Wages & Salaries	£ 19,000		
Loan Repayments	£ 0		
Insurance costs	£ 1,200		
Motor expenses	£ 0		
Petrol/ Diesel	£ 0		
Professional fees	£ 0		
Capital Equipment	£ 0		
Telephone	£ 480		
Marketing & Promotion	£ 1,200		
Consumables	£ 300		
Post and carriage	£ 0		
Printing and stationery	£ 120		
Contingencies	£ 480		
	£ 0		
	£ 0		
Total overheads	**£** **31,480**		
Operational profit before taxation		**£** **31,664**	**Calculation:** (Gross profit minus Total overheads)
Drawings (survival budget)		**£** **12,504**	
Net Profit		**£** 19,160	**Calculation:** (Operational profit before tax minus Drawings)

Chapter 4: Step 4 – Writing A Business Plan Summary:

Still with me after the mammoth business plan? In the blank template – most of the sections are straight forward and you can always refer to the example I have given.

For the cashflows, this can be tricky to work out, but the excel part will automatically work out when you have entered the data. It is formatted so you can make changes and will take out all the tough working out for adjustments.

Do not be afraid to take time to write your business plan – you need to ensure all data is accurate, you have researched your business and confident in what you are saying.

Chapter 5 – Step Five: Legal and Things To Consider

This chapter and next step might be brief, because it entirely depends on your business. I will start by saying you will seriously need to consider legal advice if purchasing or renting a shop / premises for your business.

I will say I am not in any way offering legal advice, but I decided not to use a solicitor to look over a written lease agreement for my escape room business – this had been drafted by the lease owner's solicitor and I found many mistakes whilst going over the document. Just simple things we agreed in our original meeting and in the heads of terms which I made them amend before signing.

Leasing / Heads of terms / renting premises:

If you are wanting to rent premises for your business, this is something you will agree with the owner you are wishing to rent from (or could be with a managing agent) essentially, these are terms and conditions you wish to undertake if renting premises, these terms can be verbal (I would advise you follow up any verbal heads of terms with written ones to confirm what was agreed) and will be a negotiation over rent, whether the lease is full repairing lease - a full repairing lease means that the tenant is responsible for the cost of all the repairs and upkeep of the property and the cost of buildings insurance. If the tenant occupies only part of the building these costs are usually shared with other tenants and paid in the form of a service charge.

The Heads of terms is your chance to negotiate – try not to focus only on rent, but the lease itself. Are you renting for one year? Two or three? The standard lease term is around 3 years, especially in this climate. Try to also aim for a break clause in your heads of terms which means both parties can end the contract early if agreed to do so. For example – If you take on a 3-year lease, if you have a break clause at every year, It will give you flexibility to leave if the business is not successful.

My first business, I was able to negotiate a 6-month lease which worked out well for my part as the landlord wanted to rise rent and fix in for 3 years which I was not prepared to do.

My advice is to ensure the lease will suit your business – if you are a little concerned about whether the business is viable, you could ask for a rent-free period (usually up to 6 months) which can give you an opportunity to either decorate or establish the business to see what works and what does not work. You need to seriously consider the fact that if the business fails, you will still be liable to pay the rent. No matter what happens, the rent will need to be paid and you will need a backup if you are relying on the business to pay the rent and it fails and is not able to pay it.

I was extremely lucky that I was able to start and run businesses that did succeed, but it was constantly on my mind that I needed to make enough money each day to ensure I could pay the rent and the bills.

To summarise:

Ensure you get a good deal that works for your business if you are renting premises. You will agree negotiations in the heads of terms before signing the lease.

Use a solicitor whenever possible, but if like me, you decide not to, get someone to read through the terms before you sign them. Ideally, you will agree a rent-free period and maybe a year lease.

Plan for the worst – you will be legally required to pay the rent for the business whether your business is successful or not

Business Planning Use

This is something you will need to consider if renting or buying premises. What is the business planning use for the building? All buildings fall under a Use Class defined under

The Town and Country Planning (uses classes) Order 1987 and updated in 2020 for the following:

These uses are divided into six sections. These are 'Use Class B – businesses which supply or support others', 'Use Class C – locations where people sleep', Use Class E – 'commercial, business and Service', Use Class F1 – 'learning and non-residential institutions', Use Class F2 – 'local community uses and a Sui Generis – "category for those locations which are unique in themselves".

Use Classes

Use Class B – Business that supply people

B2 – General Industrial

B8 – Storage and Distribution

Use Class C – Locations where people sleep

C1 – Hotels

C2 – Residential Institutions

C2A – Secure residential institutions

C3 – Homes

C4 – HMOs

Use Class E – Commercial, Business and Service

Various uses from shops, offices, restaurants, light industrial and much more

Use Class F1 – Learning and non-residential institutions

Schools, galleries, museums and more

Use Class F2 – Local community uses

Local Community uses

Sui Generis – meaning everything else!

If you are unsure of the use class of the building you are looking to rent for your business or service, then speak with the landlord, or managing agent. You can also speak with your local council department for planning and permission. It can take a long time for uses to be changed over, so bear in mind if you are wanting to open your business quickly. There are fines if you do not comply and change over the use. Please check anyway as these use classes may have changed.

I will say here that the local council I attempted to speak with in regards to changing the business use over for my escape room business were awful. I knew the building I was going to rent had previously been offices, so would need changing over for escape room use – but I was not sure which use class it would fall under. I contact the council beforehand and received a reply but when I replied further, I received no response. I tried many times, but the phone lines were never answered and my letters / emails were ignored.

During the pandemic, when businesses including my own were struggling the council decided I had not properly sorted the business use and that I would be required to pay for it immediately. (I think this was around £450 – I am not sure why this amount or for what it is used for, be sure to check with your local council if you can get hold of them!) I of course complained but got nowhere. I eventually sorted the business use to be converted.

Business Rates

If you are renting premises, this should have been discussed with the landlord or managing agent.

You must pay Business Rates (National Non-Domestic Rates) on properties such as shops, offices, and factories. Central Government set the multipliers (the rates in the £) each year.

The amount of business rates you will be liable for will vary depending on the rateable value of your premises. If the rateable value is £51,000 or more, you use the standard multiplier. If it is under £51,000, use the small multiplier.

For properties in England in 2023/2024 the standard multiplier has been set at 51.2p, and the small multiplier at 49.9p. Different multipliers apply if you are outside England or inside the City of London.

If your property has a rateable value of £12,000 or under, then you will be eligible to receive full small business rates relief, and you will be liable to pay no business rates. Should the rateable value fall between £12,000 and £15,000, you will receive 1% relief for every £30 the value is under £15,000. If your rateable value is £14,100, this is £900 less than £15,000, so you will receive 30% relief on your business rates bill.

There are other rate reliefs available for retail, hospitality, or leisure properties, for rural properties, for properties used for a charitable purpose or those in freeports, amongst others. Have a look at the gov.uk site on business rates relief, to see if you can qualify for a reduction. You can also speak with your local council (again if you are lucky enough to get hold of them!) about business rates for the premises you wish to trade from.

The current general revaluation for rateable values took effect from 1st April 2023, and revaluations happen regularly, so keep an eye on this!

Also, in some areas may be a part of BID – Business improvement District. When I opened my escape room business this was in a BID area. It was setup to help local business and run events, to entice people back into city centres or town centres and encourage enterprise. This is around £100 a year and cannot be opted out of if you are in a BID area.

It is good for networking, getting to know local businesses and events can help boost sales if part of a BID area.

Data Protection

This may seem daunting and you can hire professionals to help you with this, but if you wish to save money, then it is not too difficult to sort.

Data protection has majorly come into prominence in recent years – what information and data you collect from customers, along with how you store it, how long for is what you need to cover.

The best way to comply with Data Protection is to have a policy in place. You can get a template (search online), making it easier for you to fill in just what you need for your business.

You will need to add a cookies banner to your website (if you are using one), for all users (even if they do not buy anything) to browse your website. Most websites like Wix have a template you can use and simply add on. This became compulsory for all websites recently but I have heard that cookie banners are becoming annoying for users so the rule may be scrapped. Check the rules whenever you are setting something up, in case they have changed and no longer needed.

If you can safely collect, store, and then dispose of customer data you need for your business (and can demonstrate why that data is needed, such as needing a customer address to ship an item or product to them once purchased from you) it is easy enough to adhere to.

Tax

I am not an expert at this at all in fact my knowledge is very limited, usually with everything else I have done in business I suggest to do it yourself and give it a go but this time, I am not going to say that. I have an accountant to sort this for me! But it is something you will need to bear in mind if selling goods or services.

You will need to register for VAT if you start generating a turnover of £85,000 in the last 12 months (not tax year). If turnover drops below £83,000 you can de register for VAT. This may change, so be sure to check when setting up your business.

Every business expense, be it buying paper, to domains or anything you legitimately need for the business, get a receipt, and keep hold of it. You can offset expenses against tax you owe.

My advice is, record everything as efficiently as you can – each month, keep a file for expenses, for sales and if you do go down the route of hiring an accountant, they will thank you for it!

If doing it yourself, I believe Quickbooks is a good website to use but I cannot recommend.

Insurance

This goes without saying – you need insurance for your business. It will of course depend entirely what your business is, but most businesses will meet the general public, so public liability insurance will be needed. I think £5mil for PLI is the going rate (sounds like a lot but is needed for cover).

You will need to insurance to cover your premises, all stock, and anything you need for the business itself like a van or vehicle.

It is hard to advise which insurance you need without knowing what business you will be intending of opening – my best advice is to shop around and ensure you have insurance sorted beforehand of opening.

Health and Safety

If you are planning of renting premises – you will be required to adhere to all health and safety regulations.

This means, ensuring you have the correct fire extinguishers (foam or electrical etc) with labels, a fire evacuation (written) plan, the correct fire evacuation signage throughout your business premises and a meeting point in place.

You will also need to fit out fire alarms and test them regularly and show records of the tests. You will be inspected by the local fire brigade – if you are unsure on anything or need any help, contacting them beforehand and they should point you in the right direction.

A first aid kit is required on site and while it is not a legal requirement, a trained first aider would be advantageous.

Food businesses

A food business will be the most complex type of business, to ensure you meet all health and safety regulations – especially if you are to be inspected by Environmental Health. For any food business, in order to comply with Health and Safety you must:

- Register with your local council to apply 30 days before trading
- Complete level 2 in food hygiene
- Keep records of fridge / freezer temperatures
- Records of cleaning
- Records of temperature checks (need a food probe thermometer and one for backup)
- Fire safety checks

If you are using any cleaning products, be sure to check that they conform to health and safety standards especially if you are planning of opening a business that serves food and drinks. I think it is BN8509 but please check as this could change.

Chapter 6 - Step Six: Let's Start A Business – Launch

By now if you have been following the steps, you have researched your business idea, came up with the concept, thought about who you will sell to and how you will sell to them and written a full business plan. You should have sorted through all legal and health and safety requirements too.

If you have not done so already, you will have a logo (use Canva if you are wanting to do it yourself) for your business, social media setup, plus your website ready (if using one) along with marketing campaigns plans ready to go.

You may consider a launch party or something where you have giveaways, possibly to tie in with marketing the business.

Payments

Ensure you are ready for taking payments – so many businesses these days still have signs stating for 'Cash Only' –

why?! Card machines are so cheap to buy (I got mine for less than £20) and the transaction fees are usually low.

You do not want to miss any sales – I have often not purchased because of the lack of payment options as I do not carry a lot of cash around with me most of the time. And a lot of people do not:

UK Finance has published its latest Payment Markets Report, reporting on payment trends during 2021 and forecasting what we expect to happen by 2031.

40.4 billion payments were made in 2021, a return to pre-pandemic levels.

Debit cards were the most used payment method, accounting for 48 per cent of all payments.

The number of cash payments fell by 1.7 per cent in 2021, although it remained the second most used payment method, used for 15 per cent of all payments in the UK.

Faster Payments overtook Bacs Direct Credit as the payment method most frequently used by businesses.

57 per cent of UK adults used mobile banking in 2021.

Almost a third of all payments in the UK were made using contactless methods in 2021.

Obviously shop around (I would avoid renting card machines and anything that has a monthly fee), but ensure you have at least one card payment terminal up and running ready for launch. You will need to have tested it (run through dummy payments for different amounts on different payment types like Mobile payments, contactless card payments and even card payments using the long numbers and typing it in) and show customers signs that they can pay by card.

You may be providing a service, so can take a mobile card reader with you (some even allow receipts being sent via email) and have backups if in poor signal areas.

With cash payments, you need to ensure you have change (if your business is in person and requires it) you will need to pay for change at banks (pay to have money, it is crazy I know) so I used to get round this by collecting as much change as I could, ensuring any family members emptied their change so I had a build-up. Whichever way you do it, you need to have a float and count your till each morning / evening.

Sounds obvious to do, but on top of planning for everything else, it may have slipped your mind.

Checks before launch

This part depends entirely on your business and makes it difficult for me to give specific advice at this point, but I will say for you to:

- Read through and triple check your business plan, is there anything you can add to it? Will any immediate changes be needed for opening?
- Ensure socials are all updated and ready for launch
- If you have premises and it is the first day of opening – does everything look right? Is everything clean? If you have customer toilets ensure these are clean and stocked with toilet roll etc as it can put a lot of people off, you do not want to get a bad review!
- Is your till working? Card machine working? Do you have enough change
- Your website should be up and running already if you are planning to have a website but worth checking through in case of any errors
- Are opening times universal across social media, google my business and your website?
- Can you have a pretend transaction – say if you have premises, could a friend or family member come and pretend to be a customer? Or better yet, buy something from you!

Customer Service

This may sound strange, you will need to practice your customer service skills, as for most businesses, you will encounter the public, your customers in some form. This could be over the phone, face to face or virtually through email or chat. Whichever way you will be speaking to customers, it is a good idea to practice what you will say. It does not need to be scripted; it could just be a few pointers such as:

- Greeting: Good morning / afternoon etc
- Ask how the customers are doing
- If in person ask if they need any help
- Always be polite with Please / thank you.
- Be confident (sometimes easier said than done)

Obviously, you will need to be helpful, knowledgeable on your product or service and try to keep interactions light, friendly but still professional. I found being super friendly, positive and bubby with customers worked wonders in my escape room business. People even came back because of me.

You may think I am telling you how to suck eggs, but these basic customer service skills are lacking in a lot of businesses, if you get a customer, you do not want to lose them or to not return.

The same customer skills should be applied to any staff members you may have and ensure you treat every customer as if they were your last.

Negativity

With all things in life, there is a small chance of some negativity coming your way by starting a business. For example, when I opened my sweet shop – I managed to arrange a news article in the local press, which was a great for opening. But some of the comments on the article could be considered negative – comments from users about the sweet shop being unhealthy for example.

It is something I did not really expect (maybe I was a little naïve with my first business) so I dealt with the negativity as best as I could.

Not everyone will be happy for you starting a business, as I mentioned before in this book so be prepared for the worst and hopefully will not be as bad as you think.

The best way is to come up with some sort of professional response, that will be direct and handle the negativity like the reviews section below.

Reviews

Many customers came to my escape room based off our reviews. I tried to be transparent with reviews across all platforms (Google, TripAdvisor, and Facebook) and was pleased to achieve 5 stars on each.

Tie in customer service and your great products, then ask customer for a review. Simply asking them might not get anywhere but I found that mostly people who enjoyed the escape rooms would review after I had reminded them.

Reviews are not there to just gain customer feedback but often help with elevating your profile such as on google – showing your business more often on search results.

It can be difficult to gain reviews, you may ask customers like I did but even then, customers may forget or not want to. You could package in a note if sending products out, asking for the customer to review or maybe an email after they have purchased to see what their thoughts are.

You need to respond to every single review – good or bad. Hopefully you will mainly gain good reviews (simply thanking the customer for taking the time to leave a review is enough) but If you do receive a bad review – not responding is worse than tackling the situation.

Look into what the review is saying – if bad service from a staff member, then more training will be needed and apologise to the customer, stating facts that you will ensure the staff member is dealt with.

Whatever the bad review is saying – apologising and trying to make right what was wrong will be the best way forward. Be polite, be direct and honest with your response. Ensure you try to rectify the problem and explain how you will do that.

I will say, sometimes people will leave a bad review no matter what you do to ensure it does not happen – it is just the way people are. They are never happy or wanting to get a refund just because they can (or try to anyway).

The worst thing you can do is not respond or worse, respond back in a negative way. If you can find a way to make the bad review a positive situation then customers who see it will respect you as a business more.

Looking After You

This is where I keep saying that a business is hard work – it can really take its toll. I worked practically 7 days a week, day, and night to get my escape room business off the ground and my mental health suffered as a result. Also, my relationship with my husband was strained and it was not worth being in that situation, no matter the amount of money I was making.

You need to ensure that yes you work hard to make your business work but you also need to ensure you are looked after and rewarded for your work.

Use a list to split up tasks and reward yourself in whichever way you like for completing them.

Your business will thrive if you are happy plus customers can tell if you are tired, overworked or you are not yourself.

Updating your business plan

After launch, you may feel like you do not need to refer to your business plan anymore, but it can be a great tool to keep you motivated and achieve your long-term business goals.

Update the cashflows for the year, adding in any changes and making sure that you achieve better than the year before.

You want your business to grow – so writing new goals and what you will do to achieve those goals will ensure your business does this.

Keep going

Hopefully you will have friends and family helping to keep you motivated but there will be tough times you need to face.

All I can say to get through these tough times is to carry on. Keep going. Keep up plugging your social media every day and doing anything you can to always promote the business.

Keep going – you have got this!

Conclusion:

I hope my six steps to starting a business helps you. Even if it is just in a small way, as when I started, I had no idea where to begin and reading something like this would have helped me.

My reason for starting this book was to try and help others with their business, even in some small way.

Having a business is very personal, it will take over your life (unless you are looking to start something on the side rather than full time) and will be a struggle but I hope, like me, you feel like all the stress, the worry and the hard work is worth it for you. And ultimately it pays off!

I have said many times that starting a business is not easy – even if you become well established and are opening a second or even a third branch it will continue to be difficult and present new challenges with every part of the venture.

I wish you all the best in your business venture. If you can believe in yourself and work hard to achieve what you are setting out to do, you will succeed.

Keep going. It may feel like a long slog or that you are not getting anywhere fast, but keep putting in the work, keep smiling and success will come to you.

Remember to update your business plan as you move forward, write lists, and look after you. Keep updating social media and come up with new marketing campaigns to keep customers coming back and hopefully gaining new customers as well.

Please help local and small businesses in any way you can. They need you more than ever right now and every penny helps a person with a family to feed. It may sound dramatic but small businesses are becoming fewer because of a tough economic climate, because of bigger companies taking over and I for one do not want to live in a country full of the same shops, the same eateries as everywhere else. We must support the small business and help in any way we can even if that means you sharing posts on social media – it costs nothing and really helps.

Please email me if you have any questions or feedback via letsstartasomething@gmail.com
Follow me on Instagram - @letsstart.abusiness
Or threads @imamemberofstars

Glossary:

Footfall: meaning the amount of people coming to that area. This can be a little tricky to find out accurate data for, the best way would be to go to your sales area (ideally if you have a shop to be outside) and count how many people go past during a week, at different times. You will then be able to work out the average and base it over 12 months – factoring in things like seasonal changes (people buy more drinks / ice creams during warm weather for example).

Profit Margin: This is the amount you will have gained after selling your product. See Chapter one, Step one in order to work out how this is calculated.

SEO: Search Engine Optimisation – specifically referring to websites, they will be designed with SEO – certain phrases, words and search terms that search engines look for when scanning your website. This means that when a customer is looking on Google for some shoes for example, Google will bring up relevant results based on SEO from different websites for shoes (as well as how high a website would rank).

Links:

Contact Me – if you have any questions, comments or wish to speak with me for whatever reason please email letsstartasomething@gmail.com I would love to hear from you!
I am on Instagram as @letsstart.abusiness
And Threads – imamemberofstars.threads.net
Link for blank business plan for you to use:

https://tinyurl.com/BusBlank

Apps / websites / Tools I use:

Canva.com – this website is great for designing flyers, business cards, posts for social media and more. Well worth upgrading to Canva Pro (about £100 per year) if you wish to save from paying designers. Can be limited, but easy and simple to use. Before Canva, I use to use Adobe Photoshop and Illustrator which I found difficult to get to grips with, Canva has similar features and easy.

Inshot (app) – a great app for editing photos (adding in text etc). I used it a lot for posting on social media. There are free and paid versions – I did use to pay for it, but you can still use all features of the app for free but you will need to watch adverts before saving.

Facebook groups – It can be helpful to join groups based on your business. For example, when I had my escape room business, I joined Facebook groups for owners of escape rooms, groups for props used in escape rooms as well as customer-based groups such as escape room enthusiasts in the UK. Be mindful of group rules – each one is different and will not take too kindly if you are using them to advertise your business.

Local business groups – Check in your local area for a business steering group or chamber of commerce. It can be a good way to meet people and gain some insight for business in your area.

Wix – This is what I found the easiest website builder to use and you can create some nice-looking websites for low cost. You can even hire a Wix professional to do it for you (but I advise against this as it is easy for you to do yourself) with lots of templates, it can suit a wide range of businesses – extras such as e-commerce (shop) are simple to add with apps. Your domain and package can all be purchased in one price which I have found to be cheapest. The only issue I found is that while it can suit a lot of different businesses, it can be limited if you are wanting a custom site to do lots of things. Ideal for beginners – you can have a website up and running quickly.

Square Peg Insurance – ideal insurance providers if your business does easily fit into other business insurance categories. I am not saying they will be cheapest though!

YouTube – I learn by seeing things, so visual learning from videos on YouTube have helped me in the past if I have ever had a problem with my businesses. A step by step or how to can usually solve a problem If struggling. Just be wary that not all videos are done by professionals so if doing something like DIY and look to YouTube for help – it may be help or hinder.

Thank You

I would like to thank you for buying and reading my first ever book! I hope you have enjoyed it in some way and gotten something from it.

It has been a long process – I previously tried writing different novels (which I hope to go back to and complete) but could not settle on what I wanted to write.

I decided to write about what I know – and that's business. I may not be a fully qualified professional with huge businesses behind me, but I have run small businesses and made them success.

I wish to thank my husband, as once again he has stepped in to edit this book and help in so many ways. Thank you for everything you do for me and our dog, we owe you so much. I love you. X

Looking ahead

Businesses are really struggling now – both big and small. The smallest independents need your help to survive, as I have mentioned already, please shop small and local. Do your bit to keep them going.

For me, I plan to write more books in the Lets Start... series. I hope you will follow me (@letsstart.abusiness on Instagram) and possibly buy my other titles too.

I loved writing this and I do hope one day I can finish my novels I started. I would absolutely love for them to be published and see my book in a shop. It has been a dream of mine since I first read The Lord Of The Rings. I wanted to be able to create a fantasy world that would take the reader to different magical places and make them look forward to going to bed to read, like I did as a kid.

Good luck with your business venture, whatever it may be. I hope it is a success and you achieve all you set out to do.

Matthew James

About The Author

Matthew James is 34, a husband and a proud dog dad. He currently lives in the North East of England with his husband and our 3-year-old Staffordshire bull terrier named Fleur, whom they rescued last year and said it has been a joy getting to know her.

They spend our days either in the garden, walking the dog and enjoy reading or binge watching the latest shows on Netflix. He likes to being creative, likes to write and business in general.